Wraps & Ponchos
to Knit

All for easy skill level, five stylish knits offer choices to match many moods. Lacy patterns provide a hint of romance, color combos lend playfulness, and side slits are perfect for casual comfort. Yarn weights vary from bulky to fine.

LEISURE ARTS, INC. • Maumelle, Arkansas

Rectangular Lace Poncho

●●○○ EASY

SHOPPING LIST

Yarn (Medium Weight) MEDIUM 4

[5 ounces, 256 yards

(141 grams, 234 meters) per skein]:

- ☐ 4{5} skeins

Knitting Needles

Straight,

- ☐ Size 9 (5.5 mm)

  or size needed for gauge

Additional Supplies

- ☐ Yarn needle

SIZE INFORMATION

Size	Rectangle Length
Small/Medium	50" (127 cm)
Large/X-Large	59" (150 cm)
Rectangle Width	20½" (52 cm)

Size Note: We have printed the instructions for the sizes in different colors to make it easier for you to find:

- Size Small/Medium in Blue
- Size Large/X-Large in Pink

Instructions in Black apply to both sizes.

GAUGE INFORMATION

In Garter Stitch (knit every row),

16 sts and 32 rows = 4" (10 cm)

TECHNIQUES USED

- K2 tog ***(Fig. 6, page 22)***
- YO ***(Fig. 5a, page 21)***
- YO twice ***(Fig. A)***

Fig. A

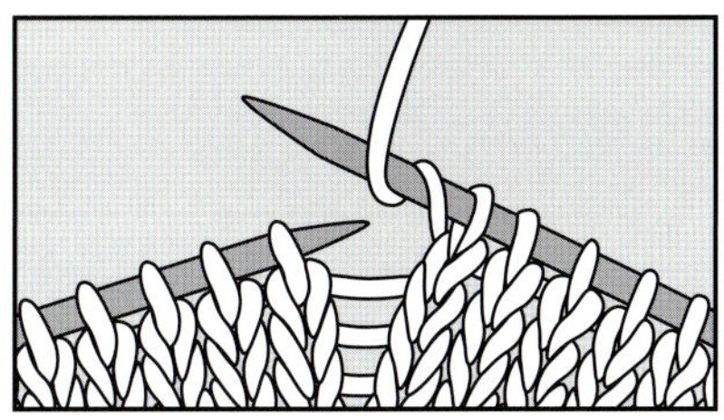

Yarn over twice counts as one stitch.

RECTANGLE

Cast on 74 sts.

Row 1: Knit across

Row 2 (Right side)**:** Knit across.

Note: Loop a short piece of yarn around any stitch to mark Row 2 as **right** side.

Row 3: K 40, (YO, K2 tog) across to last 4 sts, YO twice, K4: 75 sts.

Row 4 AND ALL RIGHT SIDE ROWS thru Row 18: K4, knit next st dropping extra YO, knit across.

Row 5: K 45, (YO, K2 tog) across to last 4 sts, YO twice, K4: 76 sts.

Row 7: K 50, (YO, K2 tog) across to last 4 sts, YO twice, K4: 77 sts.

Row 9: K 55, (YO, K2 tog) across to last 4 sts, YO twice, K4: 78 sts.

Row 11: K 60, (YO, K2 tog) across to last 4 sts, YO twice, K4: 79 sts.

Row 13: K 65, (YO, K2 tog) across to last 4 sts, YO twice, K4: 80 sts.

Row 15: K 70, (YO, K2 tog) across to last 4 sts, YO twice, K4: 81 sts.

Row 17: K 75, YO, K2 tog, YO twice, K4: 82 sts.

Row 19: Knit across.

Row 20: Bind off 8 sts in knit, knit across: 74 sts.

Repeat Rows 3-20, 20{24} times; then Repeat Rows 3-19 once **more**.

Bind off all sts in **knit**.

FINISHING

Sew cast on edge to ends of rows on the opposite side of rectangle.

Striped Poncho

●●○○ EASY

Finished Size: 29" (73.5 cm) long (neckline to tip)

SHOPPING LIST

Yarn (Bulky Weight) BULKY 5

[3.5 ounces, 127 yards (100 grams, 116 meters) per skein]:

- ☐ Brown - 2 skeins
- ☐ Green - 2 skeins
- ☐ Gold - 2 skeins
- ☐ Grey - 2 skeins

Knitting Needles

48" (122 cm) Circular,

- ☐ Size 10.5 (6.5 mm) - 2

24" (61 cm) Circular,

- ☐ Size 10.5 (6.5 mm) **or** size needed for gauge

Additional Supplies

- ☐ Stitch markers
- ☐ Point protectors

GAUGE INFORMATION

In Stockinette Stitch (knit one row, purl one row), 13 sts and 17 rows = 4" (10 cm)

TECHNIQUE USED

- Left Twist ***(Figs. 2a & b, page 20)***

PONCHO

The poncho is knit in 18 Stripes, working with 2 sets of circular needles. After each Stripe is completed, place point protectors on the tips of the needle so the piece does not unravel as you work the next Stripe.

FIRST STRIPE

With Brown and using longer circular needle, cast on 38 sts.

Row 1 (Right side)**:** P2, (Left Twist, P1) twice, knit across to last 8 sts, (P1, Left Twist) twice, P2.

Row 2: K2, (P2, K1) twice, purl across to last 8 sts, (K1, P2) twice, K2.

Rows 3-8: Repeat Rows 1 and 2, 3 times.

Cut yarn and place point protectors on needle.

SECOND STRIPE

Row 1: With **right** side of First Stripe facing, using second longer needle and Green, pick up 7 sts across ends of rows on left side of First Stripe ***(Fig. 14a, page 23)***, cast on 38 sts, pick up 7 sts across ends of rows on right side of same Stripe: 52 sts.

Row 2: K2, (P2, K1) twice, purl across to last 8 sts, (K1, P2) twice, K2.

Row 3: P2, (Left Twist, P1) twice, knit across to last 8 sts, (P1, Left Twist) twice, P2.

Rows 4-9: Repeat Rows 2 and 3, 3 times.

Cut yarn and place point protectors on needle.

THIRD STRIPE

Row 1: With **right** side of previous Stripe facing and Gold, using first circular needle, pick up 7 sts across ends of rows on previous Stripe, knit across, pick up 7 sts across ends of rows on same Stripe: 52 sts.

Row 2: K2, (P2, K1) twice, purl across to last 8 sts, (K1, P2) twice, K2.

Row 3: P2, (Left Twist, P1) twice, knit across to last 8 sts, (P1, Left Twist) twice, P2.

Rows 4-9: Repeat Rows 2 and 3, 3 times.

Cut yarn and place point protectors on needle.

FOURTH STRIPE

Row 1: With **right** side of previous Stripe facing and Grey, using second circular needle, pick up 7 sts across ends of rows on previous Stripe, knit across, pick up 7 sts across ends of rows on same Stripe: 66 sts.

Rows 2-9: Work same as Second Stripe.

Cut yarn and place point protectors on needle.

Fifth Stripe: With Green, work same as Third Stripe: 66 sts.

Sixth Stripe: With Brown, work same as Fourth Stripe: 80 sts.

Seventh Stripe: With Grey, work same as Third Stripe: 80 sts.

Eighth Stripe: With Gold, work same as Fourth Stripe: 94 sts.

Ninth Stripe: With Brown, work same as Third Stripe: 94 sts.

10th Stripe: With Green, work same as Fourth Stripe: 108 sts.

11th Stripe: Work same as Third Stripe: 108 sts.

12th Stripe: Work same as Fourth Stripe: 122 sts.

13th Stripe: With Green, work same as Third Stripe: 122 sts.

14th Stripe: With Brown, work same as Fourth Stripe: 136 sts.

15th Stripe: With Grey, work same as Third Stripe: 136 sts.

16th Stripe: With Gold, work same as Fourth Stripe: 150 sts.

17th Stripe: With Brown, work same as Third Stripe: 150 sts.

18th Stripe: With Green, work same as Fourth Stripe: 164 sts.

BOTTOM EDGING

Rnd 1: With **right** side of 18th Stripe facing and Grey, using first circular needle, pick up 7 sts across ends of rows on 18th Stripe, knit next 150 sts across 17th Stripe, pick up 7 sts across ends of rows on 18th Stripe, place marker around last st made, knit across next 164 sts (on second circular needle), place marker to indicate beginning of rnd ***(see Markers, page 20)***: 328 sts.

Rnd 2: K1, (P1, K1) across to marked st, remove marker, (P, K, P) **all** in marked st, K1, (P1, K1) across to last st, (P, K, P) **all** in last st: 332 sts.

Rnds 3 and 4: (K1, P1) around.

Bind off all sts in ribbing.

NECK EDGING

Rnd 1: With **right** side facing, Grey, and using shorter needle, pick up 74 sts evenly spaced around neck edge ***(Fig. 14b, page 23)***, place marker to indicate beginning of rnd.

Rnds 2-4: (K1, P1) around.

Bind off all sts in ribbing.

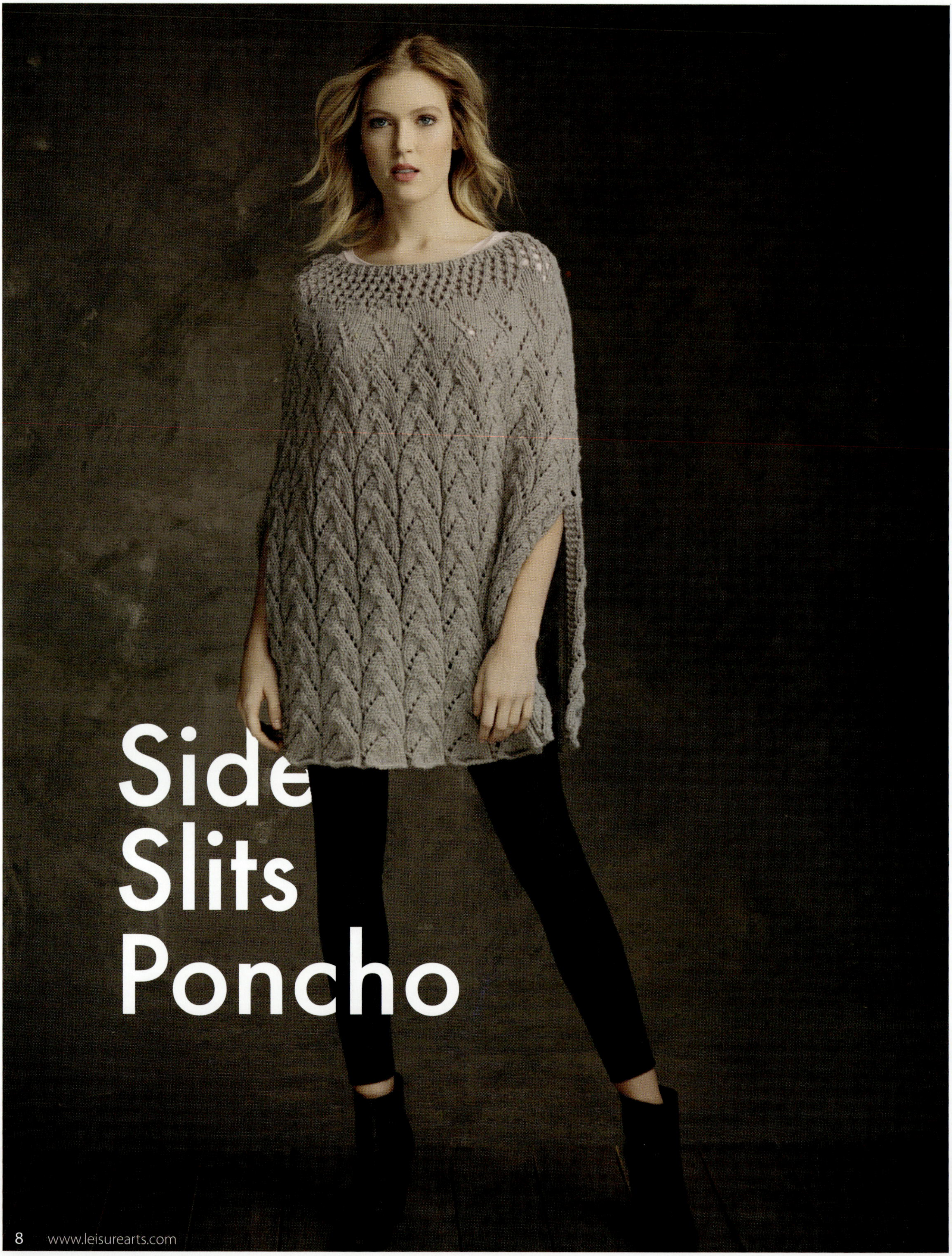

Side Slits Poncho

●●○○ EASY

SHOPPING LIST

Yarn (Bulky Weight) BULKY 5

[3.5 ounces, 153 yards (100 grams, 140 meters) per skein]:

☐ 7{8-9} skeins

Knitting Needles

24" (61 cm) Circular,

☐ Size 9 (5.5 mm) **and**

48" (122 cm) Circular,

☐ Size 10½ (6.5 mm)

or sizes needed for gauge

Additional Supplies

☐ Large stitch holder

☐ Marker

SIZE INFORMATION

Size: Small {Medium-Large}

Fits Chest Measurement:
34{42-52}"/86.5{106.5-132} cm

Finished Lower Circumference:
53½{60-66½}"/136{152.5-169} cm

Length: 29" (73.5 cm)

Size Note: We have printed the instructions for the sizes in different colors to make it easier for you to find:

- Size Small in Blue
- Size Medium in Pink
- Size Large in Green

Instructions in Black apply to all sizes.

GAUGE INFORMATION

With larger size needle, in pattern,
2 repeats (26 sts) = 6½" (16.5 cm);
20 rows = 4" (10 cm)

TECHNIQUES USED

- YO ***(Figs. 5a-c, page 21)***
- K2 tog ***(Fig. 6, page 22)***
- K3 tog ***(Fig. 7, page 22)***
- K3 tog tbl ***(Fig. 8, page 22)***
- P2 tog ***(Fig. 9, page 22)***
- Slip 1, K1, PSSO ***(Figs. 11a & b, page 22)***
- Slip 1, K2 tog, PSSO ***(Fig.12, page 23)***
- Slip 2 tog, K1, P2SSO ***(Figs. 13a & b, page 23)***

FIRST SIDE

With larger size needle, cast on 107{120-133} sts.

Row 1 (Right side)**:** K9, K2 tog, K2, YO, ★ P3, K6, K2 tog, K2, YO; repeat from ★ across to last 3 sts, K3.

Row 2 AND ALL WRONG SIDE ROWS: K3, (P 10, K3) across.

Row 3: K8, K2 tog, K2, YO, ★ K1, P3, K5, K2 tog, K2, YO; repeat from ★ across to last 4 sts, K4.

Row 5: K7, K2 tog, K2, YO, ★ K2, P3, K4, K2 tog, K2, YO; repeat from ★ across to last 5 sts, K5.

Row 7: K3, YO, K2, slip 2 tog, K1, P2SSO, K2, YO, ★ K3, P3, YO, K2, slip 2 tog, K1, P2SSO, K2, YO; repeat from ★ across to last 6 sts, K6.

Row 9: K4, YO, K2, slip 1, K1, PSSO, ★ K5, P3, K1, YO, K2, slip 1, K1, PSSO; repeat from ★ across to last 8 sts, K8.

Row 11: K5, YO, K2, slip 1, K1, PSSO, ★ K4, P3, K2, YO, K2, slip 1, K1, PSSO; repeat from ★ across to last 7 sts, K7.

Row 13: K6, YO, K2, K3 tog, K2, YO, ★ P3, K3, YO, K2, K3 tog, K2, YO; repeat from ★ across to last 3 sts, K3.

Rows 14-68: Repeat Rows 2-13, 4 times; then repeat Rows 2-8 once **more**.

Cut yarn and slip sts from needle onto st holder.

SECOND SIDE

Work same as First Side; do **not** cut yarn.

TOP

With **right** side facing, slip First Side sts from st holder to opposite end of needle. Begin working in rounds.

Rnd 1: ★ K2 tog, K2, YO, K2, slip 1, K1, PSSO, K5, † P3, K1, YO, K2, slip 1, K1, PSSO, K5 †; repeat from † to † 6{7-8} times **more**, K1, K2 tog; repeat from ★ once **more**: 210{236-262} sts.

Rnd 2: Slip first 2 sts as if to **purl**, place marker to indicate beginning of rnd ***(see Markers, page 20)***, ★ K 10, (P3, K 10) 7{8-9} times, P1, P2 tog, P1; repeat from ★ once **more**: 208{234-260} sts.

Rnd 3: ★ K2, YO, K2, slip 1, K1, PSSO, K4, P3; repeat from ★ around.

Rnd 4: (K 10, P3) around.

Rnd 5: ★ K3, YO, K2, K3 tog, K2, YO, P3; repeat from ★ around.

Rnd 6: (K 10, P3) around.

Rnd 7: ★ K5, K2 tog, K2, YO, K1, P3; repeat from ★ around.

Rnd 8: (K 10, P3) around.

Rnd 9: ★ K4, K2 tog, K2, YO, K2, P1, P2 tog; repeat from ★ around: 192{216-240} sts.

Rnd 10: (K 10, P2) around.

Rnd 11: ★ YO, K2, slip 2 tog, K1, P2SSO, K2, YO, K3, P2; repeat from ★ around.

Rnd 12: (K 10, P2) around.

Rnd 13: ★ K1, YO, K2, slip 1, K1, PSSO, K5, P2; repeat from ★ around.

Rnd 14: (K 10, P2) around.

Rnd 15: ★ K2, YO, K2, slip 1, K1, PSSO, K4, P2; repeat from ★ around.

Rnd 16: (K 10, P2) around.

Rnd 17: ★ K3, YO, K2, K3 tog, K2, YO, P2; repeat from ★ around.

Rnd 18: (K 10, P2) around.

Rnd 19: ★ K5, K2 tog, K2, YO, K1, P2 tog; repeat from ★ around: 176{198-220} sts.

Rnd 20: (K 10, P1) around.

Rnd 21: ★ K4, K2 tog, K2, YO, K2, P1; repeat from ★ around.

Rnd 22: (K 10, P1) around.

Rnd 23: ★ YO, K2, slip 2 tog, K1, P2SSO, K2, YO, K3, P1; repeat from ★ around.

Rnd 24: (K 10, P1) around.

Rnd 25: ★ K1, YO, K2, slip 1, K1, PSSO, K5, P1; repeat from ★ around.

Rnd 26: (K 10, P1) around.

Rnd 27: ★ K2, YO, K2, slip 1, K1, PSSO, K4, P1; repeat from ★ around.

Rnd 28: (K 10, P1) around.

Rnd 29: ★ K3, YO, K2, K3 tog, K1, slip 1, K1, PSSO, YO; repeat from ★ around: 160{180-200} sts.

Rnd 30 AND ALL EVEN-NUMBERED RNDS thru Rnd 56: Knit around.

Rnd 31: K5, K2 tog, K2, YO, ★ K6, K2 tog, K2, YO; repeat from ★ to last st, K1.

Rnd 33: K4, K2 tog, K2, YO, ★ K6, K2 tog, K2, YO; repeat from ★ around to last 2 sts, K2.

Rnd 35: ★ YO, K2, slip 2 tog, K1, P2SSO, K2, YO, K3; repeat from ★ around.

Rnd 37: K1, YO, K2, slip 1, K1, PSSO, ★ K6, YO, K2, slip 1, K1, PSSO; repeat from ★ around to last st, K5.

Rnd 39: K2, YO, K2, slip 1, K2 tog, PSSO, ★ K5, YO, K2, slip 1, K2 tog, PSSO; repeat from ★ around to last 3 sts, K3: 144{162-180} sts.

Rnd 41: ★ K3, YO, K2, K3 tog tbl, K1, YO; repeat from ★ around.

Rnd 43: K5, K2 tog, K1, YO, ★ K6, K2 tog, K1, YO; repeat from ★ around to last st, K1.

Rnd 45: K4, K2 tog, K1, YO, ★ K6, K2 tog, K1, YO; repeat from ★ around to last 2 sts, K2.

Rnd 47: K3, K2 tog, K1, YO, ★ K6, K2 tog, K1, YO; repeat from ★ around to last 3 sts, K3.

Rnd 49: K2, K2 tog, K1, YO, ★ K6, K2 tog, K1, YO; repeat from ★ around to last 4 sts, K4.

Rnd 51: ★ YO, slip 2 tog, K1, P2SSO, K6; repeat from ★ around: 128{144-160} sts.

Rnd 53: K1, YO, slip 1, K1, PSSO, ★ K6, YO, slip 1, K1, PSSO; repeat from ★ around to last 5 sts, K5.

Rnd 55: K2, YO, slip 1, K1, PSSO, ★ K6, YO, slip 1, K1, PSSO; repeat from ★ around to last 4 sts, K4.

Rnd 57: K3, YO, slip 1, K1, PSSO, ★ K6, YO, slip 1, K1, PSSO; repeat from ★ around to last 3 sts, K3.

Rnds 58-62: Knit around.

Rnd 63: ★ K5, K3 tog, YO; repeat from ★ around: 112{126-140} sts.

Rnds 64 and 65: Knit around.

Rnd 66: ★ K2 tog, K2, K2 tog, YO, K1, YO; repeat from ★ around.

Rnds 67 and 68: Knit around; at end of Rnd 68, remove marker.

Rnd 69: Slip next st as if to **purl**, place marker, ★ K3 tog, YO, K2 tog, YO, K2 tog, YO; repeat from ★ around: 96{108-120} sts.

Rnds 70 and 71: Knit around; at end of Rnd 71, remove marker.

Rnd 72: Slip next st as if to **purl**, place marker, (K2 tog, YO) around.

Rnds 73-75: Repeat Rnds 70-72.

Rnd 76: Knit around.

Rnd 77: (K4, K2 tog) around: 80{90-100} sts.

NECKBAND

Change to smaller size needle.

Rnds 1-3: (K1, P1) around.

Bind off all sts in K1, P1 pattern.

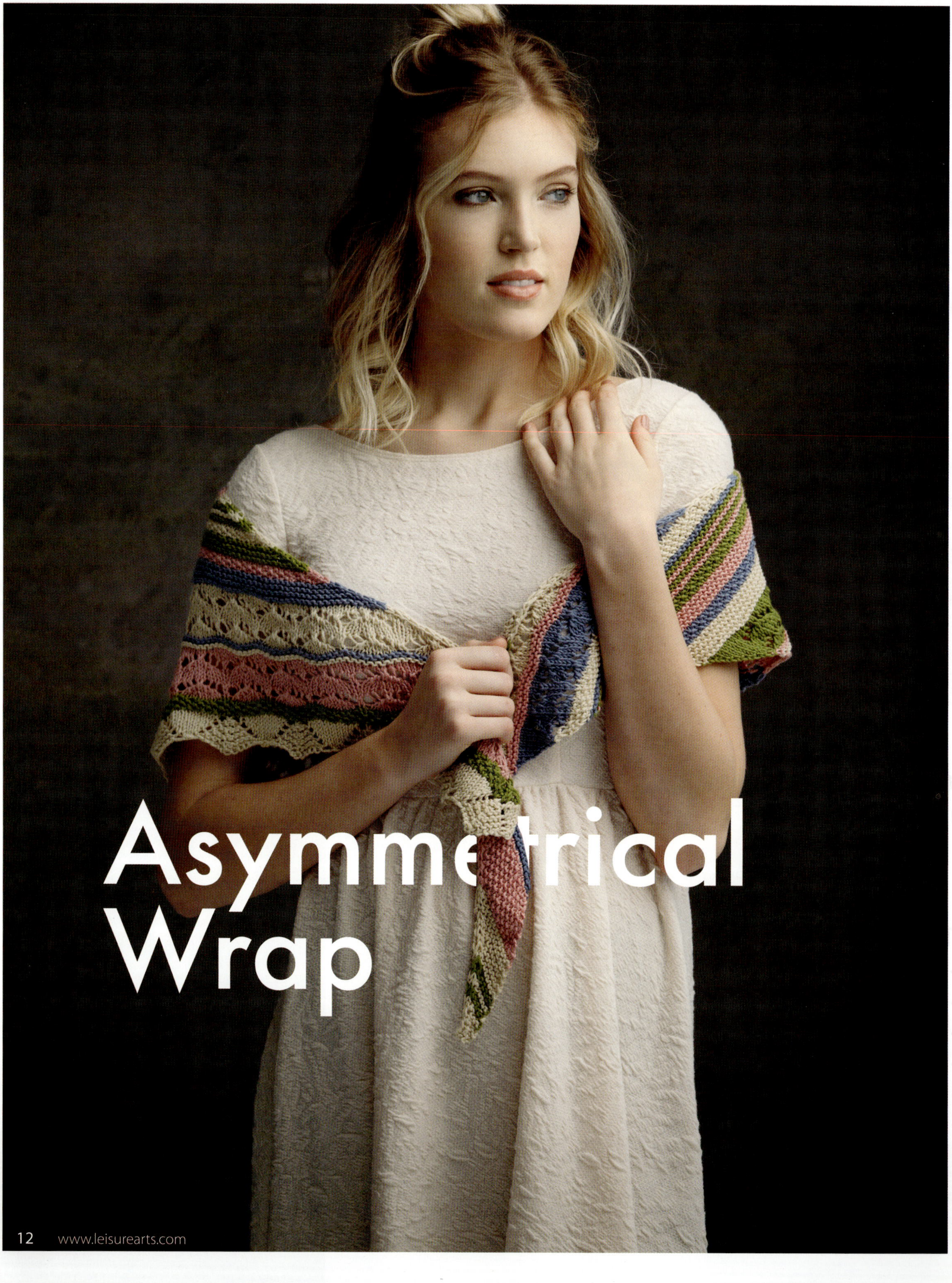

Asymmetrical Wrap

●●○○ EASY +

Finished Size: 62" long (top edge) x 27" wide (at Bottom Edge) (157.5 cm x 68.5 cm)

SHOPPING LIST

Yarn (Light Weight) LIGHT 3

[3.5 ounces, 245 yards (100 grams, 224 meters) per skein]:

- ☐ Cream - 1 skein
- ☐ Green - 1 skein
- ☐ Pink - 1 skein
- ☐ Blue - 1 skein

Knitting Needles

Straight,

- ☐ Size 6 (4 mm) **or** size needed for gauge

GAUGE INFORMATION

In Garter Stitch (knit every row), 20 sts and 40 rows = 4" (10 cm)

TECHNIQUES USED

- Knit Increase ***(Figs. 4a & b, page 21)***
- YO ***(Figs. 5a & d, page 21)***
- K2 tog ***(Fig. 6, page 22)***
- K3 tog ***(Fig. 7, page 22)***
- P2 tog ***(Fig. 9, page 22)***
- P2 tog tbl ***(Fig. 10, page 22)***
- Slip 1, K1, PSSO ***(Figs. 11a & b, page 22)***
- Slip 2 tog, K1, P2SSO ***(Figs. 13a & b, page 23)***

STITCH GUIDE

SEED STITCH *(abbreviated Seed St)*

Knit the purl stitches and purl the knit stitches as they face you.

WRAP

BOTTOM EDGE

With Cream, cast on 121 sts.

Row 1 (Right side)**:** K1, ★ YO, K4, slip 2 tog, K1, P2SSO, K4, YO, K1; repeat from ★ across.

Row 2: P2, K9, (P3, K9) across to last 2 sts, P2.

Row 3: K2, YO, K3, slip 2 tog, K1, P2SSO, K3, ★ (YO, K3) twice, slip 2 tog, K1, P2SSO, K3; repeat from ★ across to last 2 sts, YO, K2.

Row 4: P3, K7, (P5, K7) across to last 3 sts, P3.

Row 5: K3, YO, K2, slip 2, K1, P2SSO, K2, YO, ★ K5, YO, K2, slip 2 tog, K1, P2SSO, K2, YO; repeat from ★ across to last 3 sts, K3.

Row 6: P4, K5, (P7, K5) across to last 4 sts, P4.

Row 7: K4, YO, K1, slip 2 tog, K1, P2SSO, K1, YO, ★ K7, YO, K1, slip 2 tog, K1, P2SSO, K1, YO; repeat from ★ across to last 4 sts, K4.

Row 8: P5, K3, (P9, K3) across to last 5 sts, P5.

Row 9: K5, YO, slip 2 tog, K1, P2SSO, YO, ★ K9, YO, slip 2 tog, K1, P2SSO, YO; repeat from ★ across to last 5 sts, K5; cut yarn.

BODY

Row 1: With Green, purl across to last 4 sts, P2 tog, P2: 120 sts.

Row 2: K1, slip 1, K1, PSSO, K1, (P1, K1) across to last 2 sts, knit increase, K1.

Row 3 (Decrease row)**:** Work Seed St across to last 4 sts, P2 tog, P2: 119 sts.

Row 4: K1, slip 1, K1, PSSO, work Seed St across to last 2 sts, knit increase, K1.

Row 5 (Decrease row)**:** Work Seed St across to last 4 sts, P2 tog, P2; cut yarn: 118 sts.

Row 6: With Pink, K1, slip 1, K1, PSSO, knit across to last 2 sts, knit increase, K1.

Row 7 (Decrease row)**:** Purl across to last 4 sts, P2 tog, P2: 117 sts.

Row 8: K1, slip 1, K1, PSSO, ★ K1, YO, K2 tog, K3, slip 1, K1, PSSO, YO; repeat from ★ across to last 2 sts, knit increase, K1.

Row 9 (Decrease row)**:** P4, ★ † YO, P2 tog tbl, P1, P2 tog, YO †, P3; repeat from ★ across to last 9 sts, then repeat from † to † once, P2 tog, P2: 116 sts.

Row 10: K1, slip 1, K1, PSSO, K1, YO, slip 2 tog, K1, P2SSO, YO, ★ K5, YO, slip 2 tog, K1, P2SSO, YO; repeat from ★ across to last 5 sts, K3, knit increase, K1.

Row 11 (Decrease row)**:** Purl across to last 4 sts, P2 tog, P2: 115 sts.

Row 12: K1, slip 1, K1, PSSO, knit across to last 2 sts, knit increase, K1.

Row 13 (Decrease row)**:** Purl across to last 4 sts, P2 tog, P2: 114 sts.

Row 14: K1, slip 1, K1, PSSO, K3, YO, K2 tog, K3, slip 1, K1, PSSO, YO, ★ K1, YO, K2 tog, K3, slip 1, K1, PSSO, YO; repeat from ★ across to last 5 sts, K3, knit increase, K1.

Row 15 (Decrease row)**:** P7, YO, P2 tog tbl, P1, P2 tog, YO, ★ P3, YO, P2 tog tbl, P1, P2 tog, YO; repeat from ★ across to last 6 sts, P2, P2 tog, P2: 113 sts.

Row 16: K1, slip 1, K1, PSSO, K3, YO, slip 2 tog, K1, P2SSO, YO, ★ K5, YO, slip 2 tog, K1, P2SSO, YO; repeat from ★ across to last 8 sts, K6, knit increase, K1.

Row 17 (Decrease row)**:** Purl across to last 4 sts, P2 tog, P2; cut yarn: 112 sts.

Row 18: With Cream, K1, slip 1, K1, PSSO, knit across to last 2 sts, knit increase, K1.

Row 19 (Decrease row)**:** Knit across to last 3 sts, P2 tog, P1; cut yarn: 111 sts.

Rows 20 and 21: With Blue, repeat Rows 18 and 19: 110 sts.

Rows 22-33: With Cream, repeat Rows 6-17: 104 sts.

Row 34: With Blue, K1, slip 1, K1, PSSO, knit across to last 2 sts, knit increase, K1.

Row 35 (Decrease row)**:** Knit across to last 3 sts, P2 tog, P1: 103 sts.

Rows 36-41: Repeat Rows 34 and 35, 3 times; at end of Row 41, cut yarn: 100 sts.

Row 42: With Pink, K1, slip 1, K1, PSSO, knit across to last 2 sts, knit increase, K1.

Rows 43-45: Repeat Rows 3-5: 98 sts.

Rows 46-51: With Green, repeat Rows 34 and 35, 3 times; at end of Row 51, cut yarn: 95 sts.

Rows 52-55: With Cream, repeat Rows 42-45: 93 sts.

Rows 56-65: Repeat Rows 18 and 19, 5 times in the following color sequence - 2 rows **each**: (Green, Cream) twice, Pink: 88 sts.

Row 66: With Blue, K1, slip 1, K1, PSSO, knit across to last 2 sts, knit increase, K1.

Row 67 (Decrease row)**:** Work Seed St across to last 4 sts, P2 tog, P2: 87 sts.

Row 68: K1, slip 1, K1, PSSO, work Seed St across to last 2 sts, knit increase, K1.

Rows 69-86: Repeat Rows 67 and 68, 9 times; at end of Row 86, cut yarn: 78 sts.

Rows 87-97: With Pink, repeat Rows 7-17: 72 sts.

Rows 98-101: Repeat Rows 18 and 19 twice in the following color sequence - 2 rows **each**: Cream and Pink: 70 sts.

Rows 102-113: With Green, repeat Rows 6-17: 64 sts.

Rows 114-121: With Cream, repeat Rows 34 and 35, 4 times; at end of Row 121, cut yarn: 60 sts.

Rows 122-125: With Blue, repeat Rows 2-5: 58 sts.

Rows 126-131: With Pink, repeat Rows 34 and 35, 3 times; at end of Row 131, cut yarn: 55 sts.

Rows 132-135: With Green, repeat Rows 2-5: 53 sts.

Rows 136-145: Repeat Rows 18 and 19, 5 times in the following color sequence - 2 rows **each**: (Pink, Green) twice, Blue: 48 sts.

Rows 146-149: With Cream, repeat Rows 2-5: 46 sts.

Rows 150-161: With Blue, repeat Rows 6-17: 40 sts.

Rows 162-165: With Pink, repeat Rows 34 and 35 twice; at end of Row 165, cut yarn: 38 sts.

Rows 164-177: With Cream, repeat Rows 6-17: 32 sts.

Rows 178-181: With Green, repeat Rows 34 and 35 twice; at end of Row 181, cut yarn: 30 sts.

Rows 182-191: Repeat Rows 18 and 19, 5 times in the following color sequence - 2 rows **each**: Pink, Green, Pink, Blue, Pink: 25 sts.

Rows 192-195: With Blue, repeat Rows 34 and 35 twice; at end of Row 195, cut yarn: 23 sts.

Row 196: With Pink, K1, slip 1, K1, PSSO, knit across to last 2 sts, knit increase, K1.

Rows 197-208: Repeat Rows 67 and 68, 6 times; at end of Row 208, cut yarn: 17 sts.

Row 209: With Cream, purl across to last 4 sts, P2 tog, P2: 16 sts.

Rows 210-217: Repeat Rows 34 and 35, 4 times; at end of Row 217, cut yarn: 12 sts.

Rows 218-223: Repeat Rows 18 and 19, 3 times in the following color sequence - 2 rows **each**: Green, Cream, Green: 9 sts.

Rows 224-231: With Cream, repeat Rows 34 and 35, 4 times; do **not** cut yarn: 5 sts.

Row 232: K1, slip 1, K1, PSSO, knit increase, K1.

Row 233: K2, P2 tog, P1: 4 sts.

Row 234: K1, slip 1, K1, PSSO, K1: 3 sts.

Row 235: K3tog; cut yarn and pull through last st.

Textured Wrap

●●○○ EASY

Finished Size: 20" x 59" (51 cm x 150 cm)

SHOPPING LIST

Yarn (Fine Weight) FINE 2

[3 ounces, 380 yards (85 grams, 348 meters) per skein]:

☐ 4 skeins

Knitting Needles

Straight,

☐ Size 8 (5 mm) **or** size needed for gauge

GAUGE INFORMATION

Holding 2 strands of yarn together, in Stockinette Stitch (knit one row, purl one row), 16 sts and 22 rows = 4" (10 cm)

TECHNIQUES USED

- Right Twist ***(Figs. 1a & b, page 20)***
- Left Twist ***(Figs. 2a & b, page 20)***
- M1 ***(Figs. 3a & b, page 20)***
- K2 tog ***(Fig. 6, page 22)***

BOTTOM RIBBING

Holding 2 strands of yarn together, cast on 84 sts.

Rows 1-4: (K1, P1) across.

BODY

Row 1 (Right side)**:** P1, ★ † Right Twist, Left Twist, P4, Left Twist †, M1, K 14; repeat from ★ 2 times **more**, then repeat from † to † once, P1: 87 sts.

Row 2 AND ALL WRONG SIDE ROWS: Purl across.

Row 3: P1, ★ † Right Twist, P1, Left Twist, P3, Left Twist †, K 15; repeat from ★ 2 times **more**, then repeat from † to † once, P1.

Row 5: P1, ★ † Right Twist, (P2, Left Twist) twice †, K 15; repeat from ★ 2 times **more**, then repeat from † to † once, P1.

Row 7: P1, ★ † Right Twist, P3, Left Twist, P1, Left Twist †, K 15; repeat from ★ 2 times **more**, then repeat from † to † once, P1.

Row 9: P1, ★ † Right Twist, P4, Left Twist twice †, K 15; repeat from ★ 2 times **more**, then repeat from † to † once, P1.

Row 11: P1, ★ † Right Twist, P5, K1, Left Twist †, K 15; repeat from ★ 2 times **more**, then repeat from † to † once, P1.

Row 13: P1, ★ † Right Twist, P4, Right Twist, Left Twist †, K 15; repeat from ★ 2 times **more**, then repeat from † to † once, P1.

Row 15: P1, ★ † Right Twist, P3, Right Twist, P1, Left Twist †, K 15; repeat from ★ 2 times **more**, then repeat from † to † once, P1.

Row 17: P1, ★ † (Right Twist, P2) twice, Left Twist †, K 15; repeat from ★ 2 times **more**, then repeat from † to † once, P1.

Row 19: P1, ★ † Right Twist, P1, Right Twist, P3, Left Twist †, K 15; repeat from ★ 2 times **more**, then repeat from † to † once, P1.

Row 21: P1, ★ † Right Twist twice, P4, Left Twist †, K 15; repeat from ★ 2 times **more**, then repeat from † to † once, P1.

Row 23: P1, ★ † Right Twist, Left Twist, P4, Left Twist †, K 15; repeat from ★ 2 times **more**, then repeat from † to † once, P1.

Repeat Rows 2-23 for pattern until piece measures approximately 58" (147.5 cm) from cast on edge, ending by working Row 22.

Next Row: P1, ★ † Right Twist, Left Twist, P4, Left Twist †, K2 tog, K 13; repeat from ★ 2 times **more**, then repeat from † to † once, P1: 84 sts.

Last Row: Purl across.

TOP RIBBING

Rows 1-4: (K1, P1) across.

Bind off all sts in ribbing.

General Instructions

ABBREVIATIONS

cm	centimeters
K	knit
M1	make one
mm	millimeters
P	purl
PSSO	pass slipped stitch over
P2SSO	pass 2 slipped stitches over
Rnd(s)	Round(s)
st(s)	stitch(es)
tbl	through back loop(s)
tog	together
YO	yarn over

SYMBOLS & TERMS

★ — work instructions following ★ as many **more** times as indicated in addition to the first time.

† to † — work all instructions from first † to second † **as many** times as specified.

( ) or **[ ]** — work enclosed instructions **as many** times as specified by the number immediately following **or** work all enclosed instructions in the stitch indicated **or** contains explanatory remarks.

colon (:) — the number(s) given after a colon at the end of a row or round denote(s) the number of stitches you should have on that row or round.

KNIT TERMINOLOGY		
UNITED STATES		INTERNATIONAL
gauge	=	tension
bind off	=	cast off
yarn over (YO)	=	yarn forward (yfwd) **or** yarn around needle (yrn)

Yarn Weight Symbol & Names	LACE 0	SUPER FINE 1	FINE 2	LIGHT 3	MEDIUM 4	BULKY 5	SUPER BULKY 6	JUMBO 7
Type of Yarns in Category	Fingering, size 10 crochet thread	Sock, Fingering, Baby	Sport, Baby	DK, Light Worsted	Worsted, Afghan, Aran	Chunky, Craft, Rug	Super Bulky, Roving	Jumbo, Roving
Knit Gauge Ranges in Stockinette St to 4" (10 cm)	33-40 sts**	27-32 sts	23-26 sts	21-24 sts	16-20 sts	12-15 sts	7-11 sts	6 sts and fewer
Advised Needle Size Range	000 to 1	1 to 3	3 to 5	5 to 7	7 to 9	9 to11	11 to 17	17 and larger

* GUIDELINES ONLY: The chart above reflects the most commonly used gauges and needle sizes for specific yarn categories.

** Lace weight yarns are usually knitted on larger needles to create lacy openwork patterns. Accordingly, a gauge range is difficult to determine. Always follow the gauge stated in your pattern.

●○○○ **BEGINNER**	Projects for first-time knitters using basic knit and purl stitches. Minimal shaping.
●●○○ **EASY**	Projects using basic stitches, repetitive stitch patterns, simple color changes, and simple shaping and finishing.
●●●○ **INTERMEDIATE**	Projects with a variety of stitches, such as basic cables and lace, simple intarsia, double-pointed needles and knitting in the round needle techniques, mid-level shaping and finishing.
●●●● **EXPERIENCED**	Projects using advanced techniques and stitches, such as short rows, fair isle, more intricate intarsia, cables, lace patterns, and numerous color changes.

KNITTING NEEDLES																			
U.S.	0	1	2	3	4	5	6	7	8	9	10	10½	11	13	15	17	19	35	50
U.K.	13	12	11	10	9	8	7	6	5	4	3	2	1	00	000	---	---	---	---
Metric - mm	2	2.25	2.75	3.25	3.5	3.75	4	4.5	5	5.5	6	6.5	8	9	10	12.75	15	19	25

GAUGE

Exact gauge is **essential** for proper size. Before beginning your project, make a sample swatch with the yarn and needle specified. After completing the swatch, measure it, counting your stitches and rows carefully. If your swatch is larger or smaller than specified, **make another, changing needle size to get the correct gauge**. Keep trying until you find the size needles that will give you the specified gauge. Once proper gauge is obtained, measure width of garment approximately every 3" (7.5 cm) to be sure gauge remains consistent.

MARKERS

As a convenience to you, we have used markers to help distinguish the beginning of a pattern or a round. Place markers as instructed. You may use purchased markers or tie a length of contrasting color yarn around the needle. When you reach a marker on each row or round, slip it from the left needle to the right needle; remove it when no longer needed.

RIGHT TWIST

Knit second stitch on left needle ***(Fig. 1a)*** making sure **not** to drop off, then knit the first stitch ***(Fig. 1b)*** letting both sts drop off needle together.

Fig. 1a

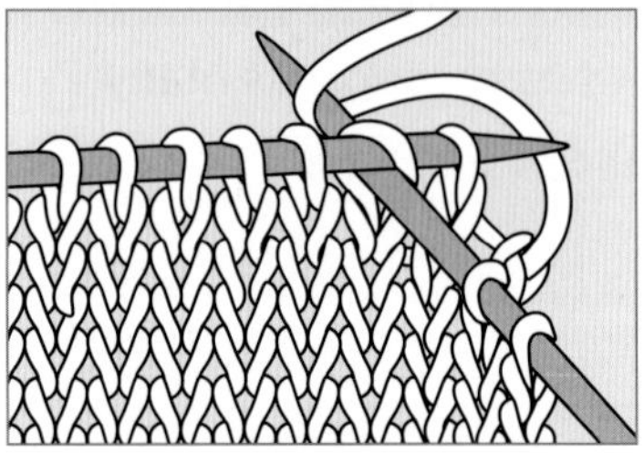

Fig. 1b

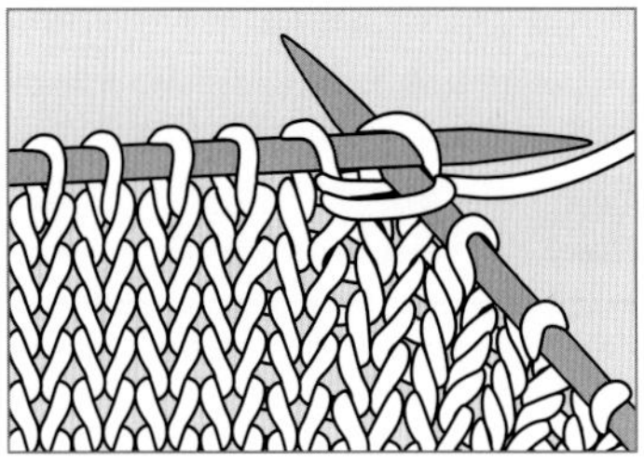

LEFT TWIST

Working **behind** first st on left needle, knit into the back of second st ***(Fig. 2a)*** making sure **not** to drop off, then knit the first st ***(Fig. 2b)*** letting both sts drop off needle.

Fig. 2a

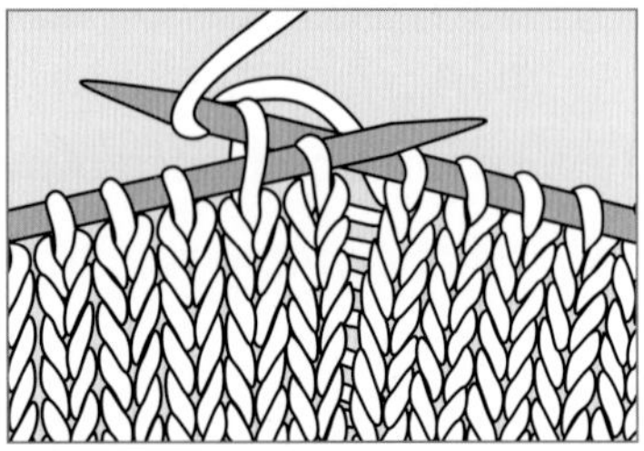

Fig. 2b

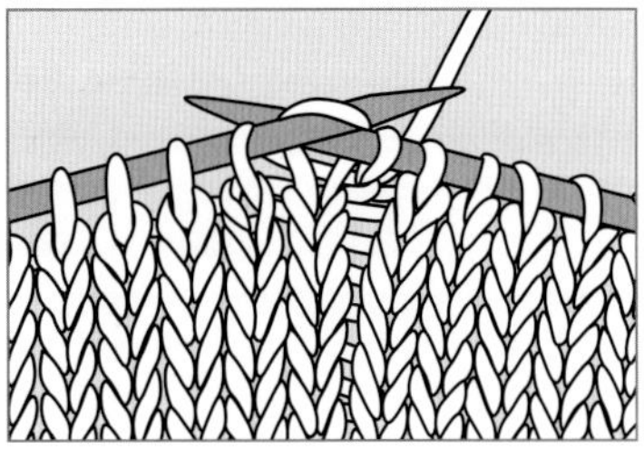

INCREASES

MAKE ONE *(abbreviated M1)*

Insert the **left** needle under the horizontal strand between the stitches from the front ***(Fig. 3a)***. Then knit into the **back** of the strand ***(Fig. 3b)***.

Fig. 3a

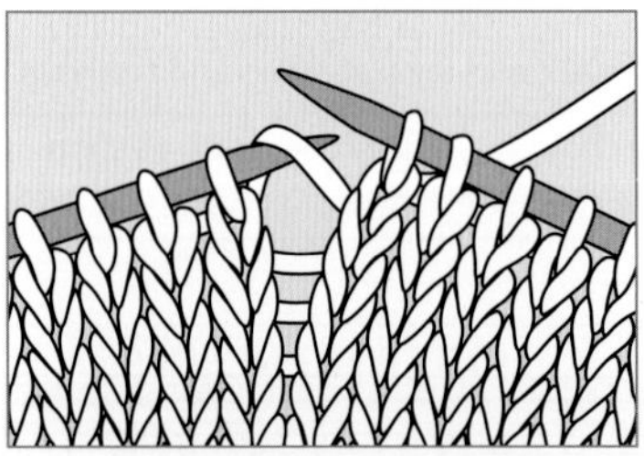

Fig. 3b

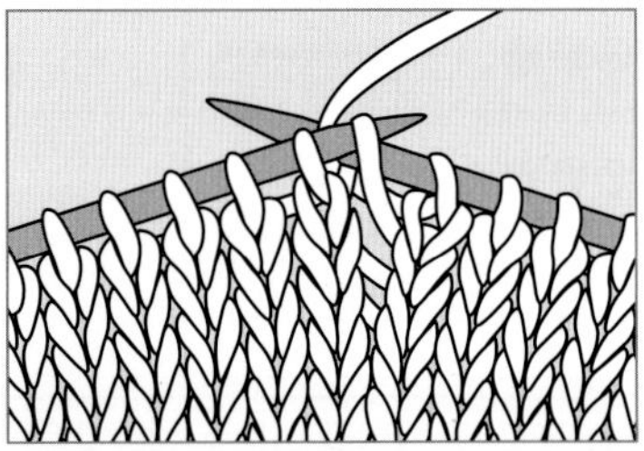

KNIT INCREASE

Knit the next stitch but do **not** slip the old stitch off the left needle ***(Fig. 4a)***. Insert the right needle into the **back** loop of the **same** stitch and knit it ***(Fig. 4b)***, then slip the old stitch off the left needle.

Fig. 4a

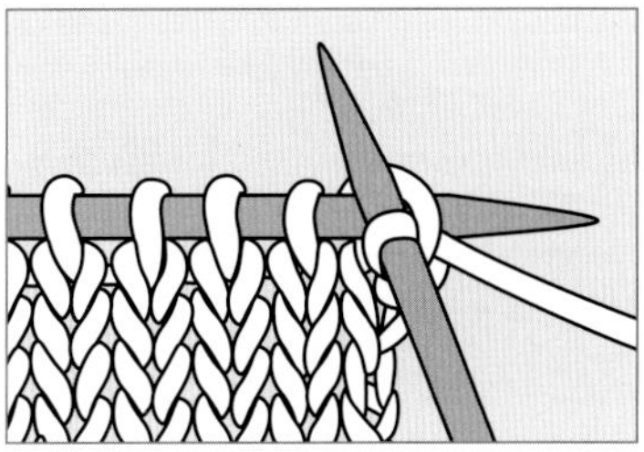

Fig. 4b

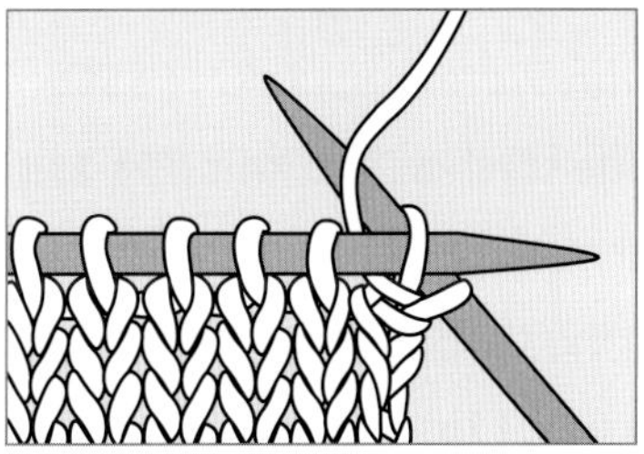

YARN OVER *(abbreviated YO)*

After a knit stitch, before a knit stitch

Bring the yarn forward **between** the needles, then back **over** the top of the right needle, so that it is now in position to knit the next stitch ***(Fig. 5a)***.

Fig. 5a

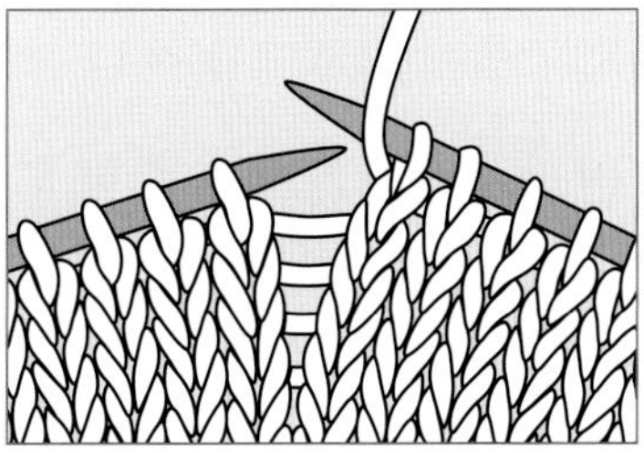

After a knit stitch, before a purl stitch

Bring yarn forward **between** the needles, then back **over** the top of the hand needle and forward **between** the needles again, so that it is now in position to purl the next stitch ***(Fig. 5b)***.

Fig. 5b

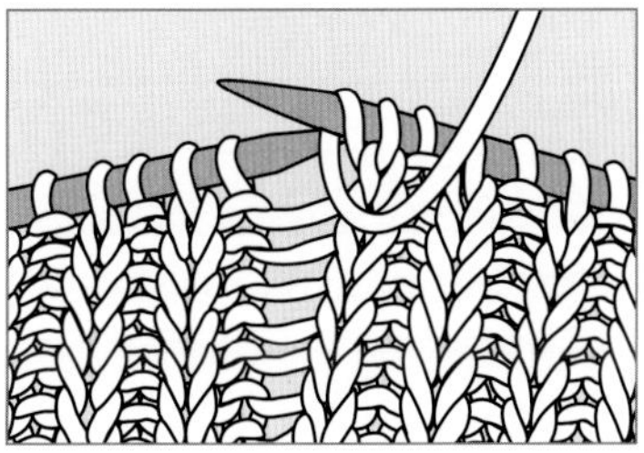

After a purl stitch, before a knit stitch

Take yarn **over** right needle to the back, so that it is now in position to knit the next stitch ***(Fig. 5c)***.

Fig. 5c

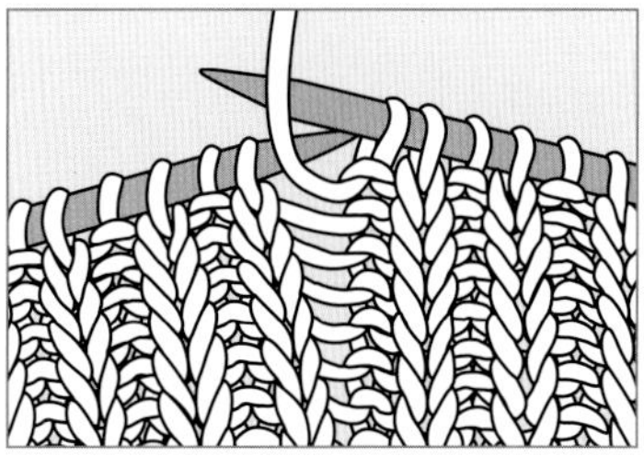

After a purl stitch, before a purl stitch

Take yarn **over** the right needle to the back, then forward under it, so that it is now in position to purl the next stitch ***(Fig. 5d)***.

Fig. 5d

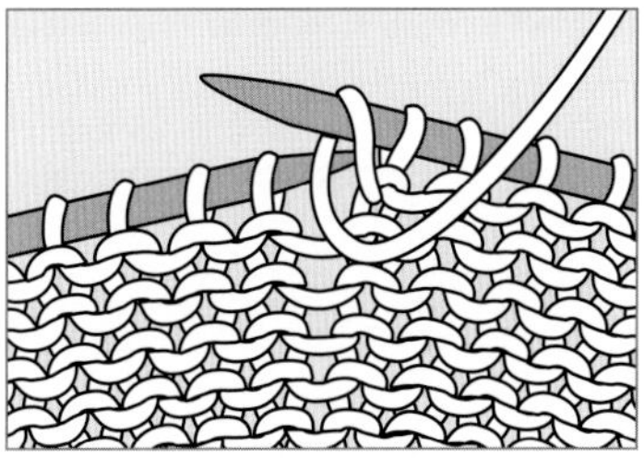

DECREASES

KNIT 2 TOGETHER

(abbreviated K2 tog)

Insert the right needle into the **front** of the first two stitches on the left needle as if to **knit** ***(Fig. 6)***, then **knit** them together as if they were one stitch.

Fig. 6

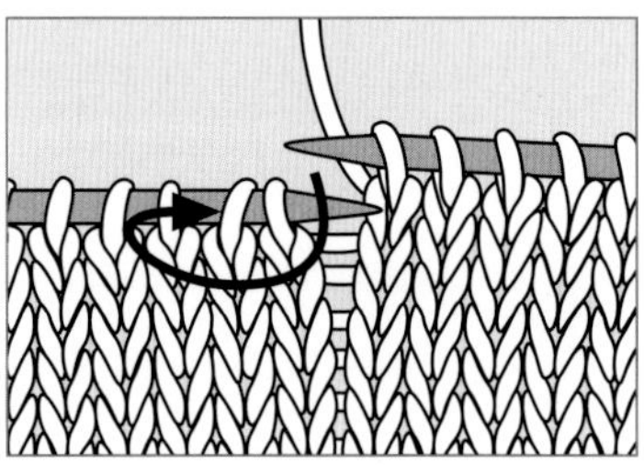

KNIT 3 TOGETHER

(abbreviated K3 tog)

Insert the right needle into the **front** of the first three stitches on the left needle as if to **knit** ***(Fig. 7)***, then **knit** them together as if they were one stitch.

Fig. 7

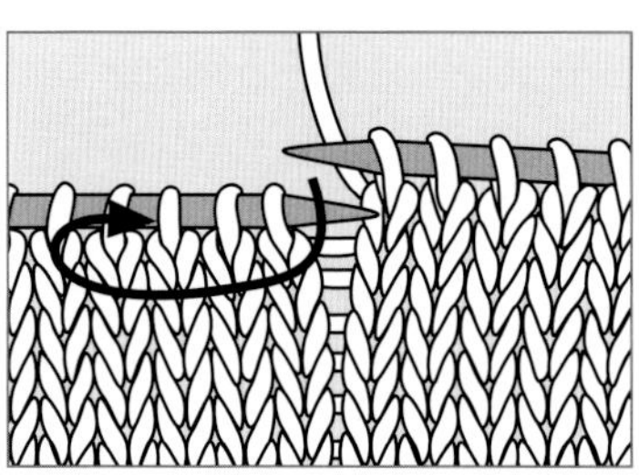

KNIT 3 TOGETHER THROUGH BACK LOOP

(abbreviated K3 tog tbl)

Insert the right needle into the **back** of first three stitches on the left needle from **front** to **back** ***(Fig. 8)***, then **knit** them together as if they were one stitch.

Fig. 8

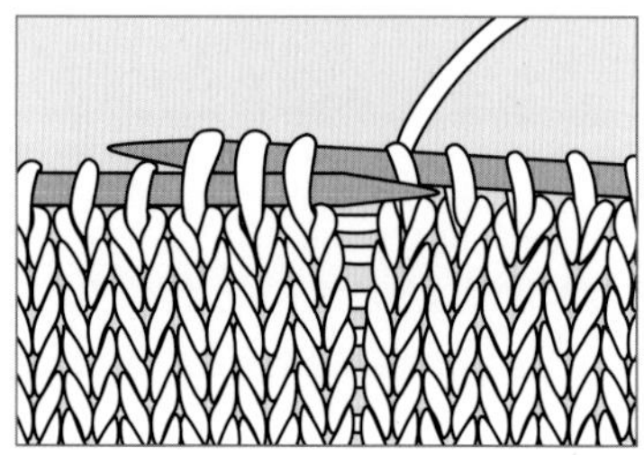

PURL 2 TOGETHER

(abbreviated P2 tog)

Insert the right needle into the **front** of the first two stitches on the left needle as if to **purl** ***(Fig. 9)***, then **purl** them together as if they were one stitch.

Fig. 9

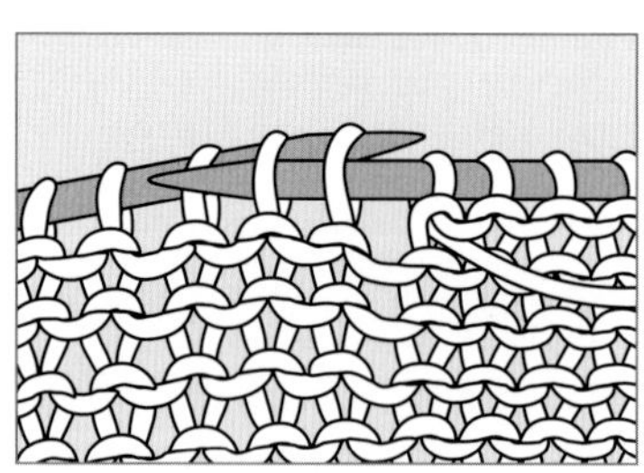

PURL 2 TOGETHER THROUGH THE BACK LOOP

(abbreviated P2 tog tbl)

Insert the right needle into the **back** of first two stitches from **back** to **front** ***(Fig. 10)***, then **purl** them together as if they were one stitch.

Fig. 10

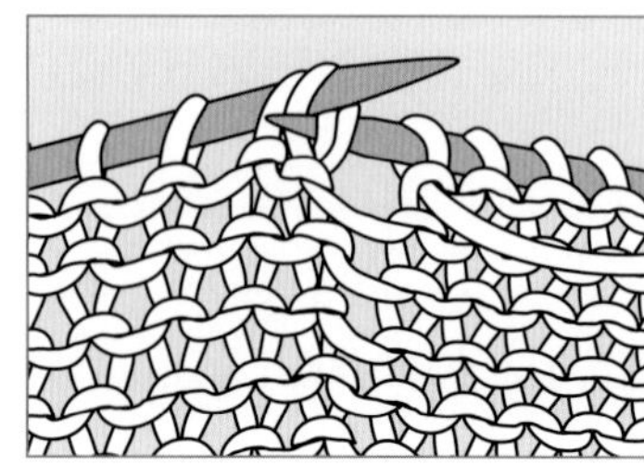

SLIP 1, KNIT 1, PASS SLIPPED STITCH OVER

(abbreviated slip 1, K1, PSSO)

Slip one stitch as if to **knit** ***(Fig. 11a)***. Knit the next stitch. With the left needle, bring the slipped stitch over the knit stitch ***(Fig. 11b)*** and off the needle.

Fig. 11a

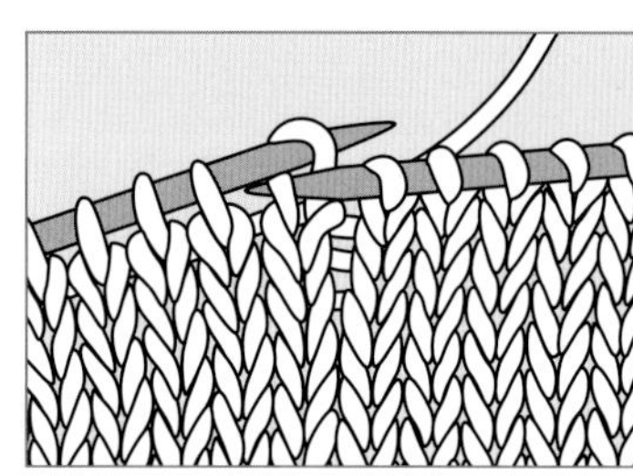

Fig. 11b

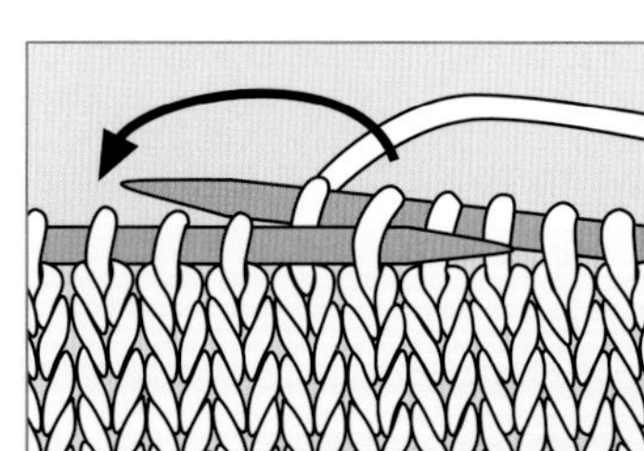

SLIP 1, KNIT 2 TOGETHER, PASS SLIPPED STITCH OVER

(abbreviated slip 1, K2 tog, PSSO)

Slip one stitch as if to **knit** ***(Fig. 11a, page 22)***, then knit the next two stitches together ***(Fig. 6, page 22)***. With the left needle, bring the slipped stitch over the stitch just made ***(Fig. 12)*** and off the needle.

Fig. 12

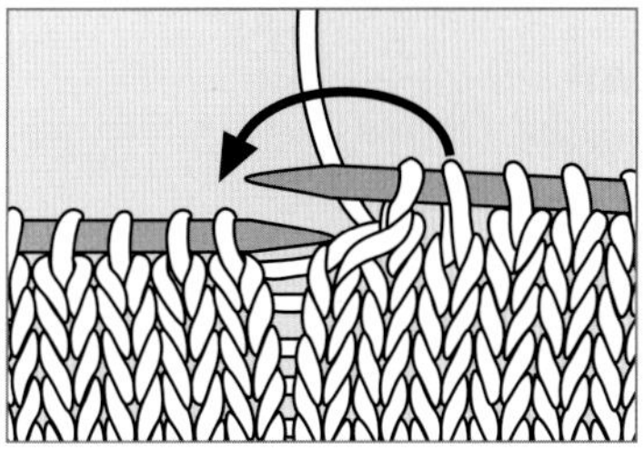

SLIP 2 TOGETHER, KNIT 1, PASS 2 SLIPPED STITCHES OVER

(abbreviated slip 2 tog, K1, P2SSO)

Slip next 2 stitches together as if to **knit** ***(Fig. 13a)***. Knit the next stitch. With the left needle, bring the slipped stitches over the stitch just made ***(Fig. 13b)*** and off the needle.

Fig. 13a

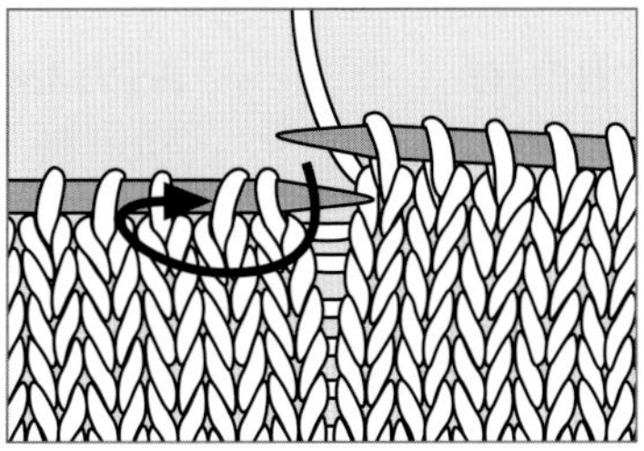

Fig. 13b

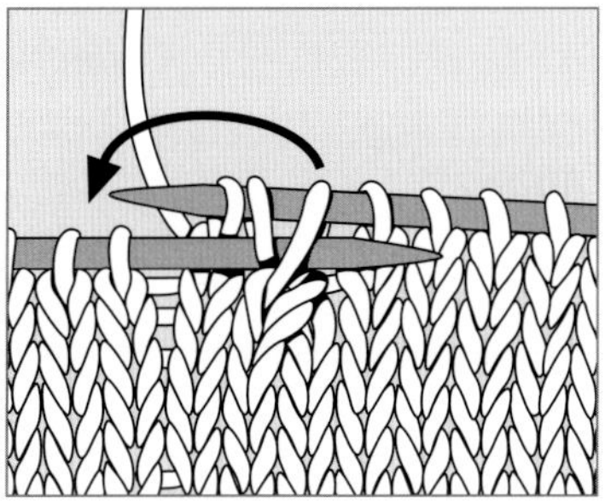

PICKING UP STITCHES

When instructed to pick up stitches, insert the needle from the **front** to the **back** under two strands at the edge of the worked piece ***(Figs. 14a & b)***. Put the yarn around the needle as if to **knit**, then bring the needle with the yarn back through the stitch to the right side, resulting in a stitch on the needle.

Repeat this along the edge, picking up the required number of stitches. A crochet hook may be helpful to pull yarn through.

Fig. 14a

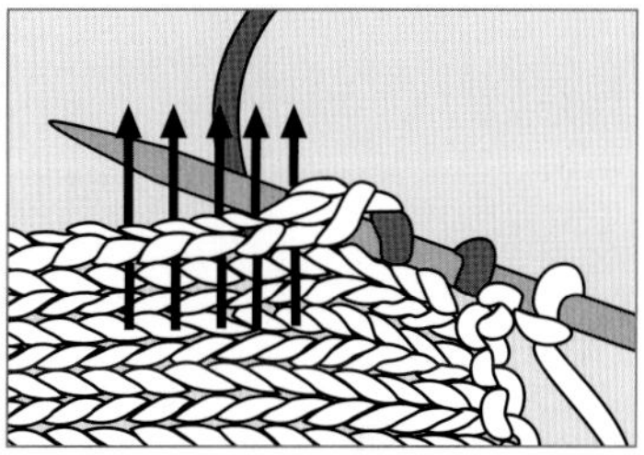

Fig. 14b

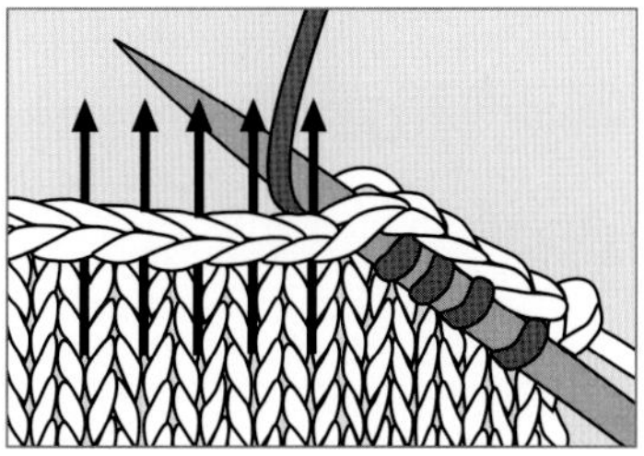

Yarn Information

The items in this book were made using a variety of yarns. Any brand of the specific weight of yarn may be used. It is best to refer to the yardage/meters when determining how many balls or skeins to purchase. Remember, to arrive at the finished size, it is the GAUGE/TENSION that is important, not the brand of yarn.

For your convenience, listed below are the specific yarns used to create our photography models. Because yarn manufacturers make frequent changes to their product lines, you may sometimes find it necessary to use a substitute yarn or to search for the discontinued product at alternate suppliers (locally or online).

RECTANGULAR LACE PONCHO
Red Heart® Soft®
#4601 Off White

STRIPED PONCHO
Lion Brand® Lion's Pride® Woolspun®
Brown - #126 Coffee
Green - #170 Peacock
Gold - #130 Honey
Grey - #149 Charcoal

SIDE SLITS PONCHO
Premier Yarns® Downton Abbey™ Collection Branson
#08 Vapor Grey

ASYMMETRICAL WRAP
Lion Brand® LB Collection® Cotton Bamboo
Cream - #098 Magnolia
Green - #174 Snapdragon
Pink - #102 Cherry Blossom
Blue - #107 Hyacinth

TEXTURED WRAP
Premier Yarns® Downton Abbey™ Collection Lady Sybil
#02 Pearl Pink

We have made every effort to ensure that these instructions are accurate and complete. We cannot, however, be responsible for human error, typographical mistakes, or variations in individual work.

Production Team: Instructional/ Technical Editor - Sarah J. Green; Editorial Writer - Susan Frantz Wiles; Senior Graphic Artist - Lora Puls; Graphic Artist - Victoria Temple; Photo Stylist - Lori Wenger; and Photographer - Jason Masters.